W9-AYC-458

THE PAPER DOORWAY

DEAN KOONTZ
THE PAPER DOORWAY
FUNNY VERSE AND NOTHING WORSE

Illustrated by Phil Parks

HARPERTROPHY®
An Imprint of HarperCollinsPublishers

Harper Trophy® is a registered trademark of HarperCollins Publishers Inc.

The Paper Doorway
Copyright © 2001 by Dean Koontz and Phil Parks
All rights reserved. No part of this book may be used or reproduced in any manner
whatsoever without written permission except in the case of brief quotations embodied in
critical articles and reviews. Printed in the United States of America. For information address
HarperCollins Children's Books, a division of HarperCollins Publishers,
1350 Avenue of the Americas, New York, NY 10019.

Library of Congress Cataloging-in-Publication Data
Koontz, Dean R. (Dean Ray).
  The paper doorway : funny verse and nothing worse / Dean Koontz ;
illustrated by Phil Parks.
      p.   cm.
  ISBN 0-06-029488-4 — ISBN 0-06-029489-2 (lib. bdg.) — ISBN 0-06-440984-8 (pbk.)
  1. Children's poetry, American.   2. Humorous poetry, American.   [1. Humorous poetry.
2. American poetry.]   I. Parks, Phil, ill.   II. Title.
PS3561.O55 P36   2001   2001024718
811'.54—dc21   CIP
                                                                                    AC

Typography by Robbin Gourley

First Harper Trophy edition, 2003

Visit us on the World Wide Web!
www.harperchildrens.com

To Gerda, whose heart I won, in part,
because I wooed her with funny verse
—D.K.

For Cynthia, all my love and then some
—P.P.

THE PAPER DOORWAY

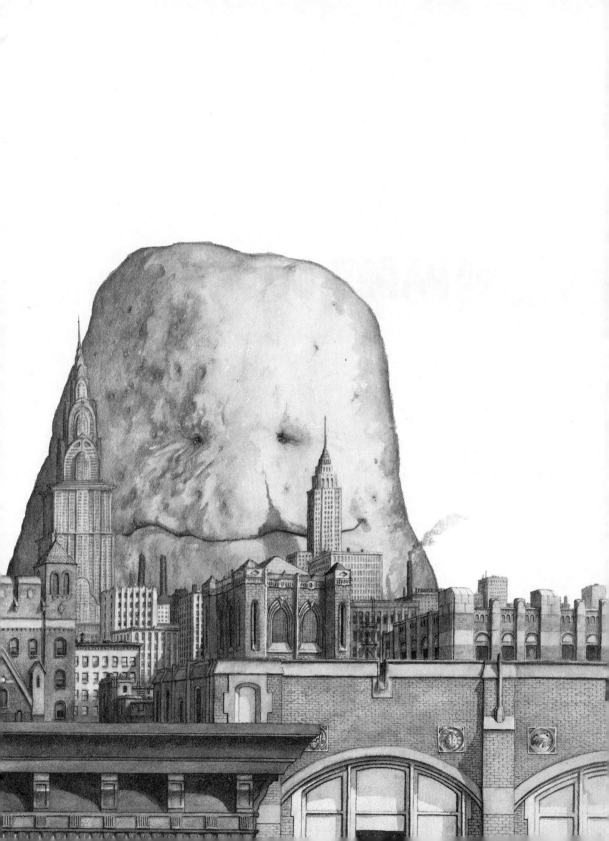

IF I WERE A POTATO

If I were a potato—you know?—
I'd grow and grow, grow and grow,
From here to there, there to here,
Until people came from far and near
To see a potato as big as a boat.
I'd be proud, but I wouldn't gloat.
I'd quietly grow bigger, bigger,
Until no one on earth could figure
What my precise weight might be—
Until I was bigger than New Jersey.
People would be dumbstruck with awe,
Eyes wide in wonder, gaping jaws.
Some would say, "What's so great?
Just a potato of enormous weight."
But nothing they say could hurt
My feelings as I lay in the dirt,
Because no potato could ever be
A bigger or better potato than me.
A potato couldn't claim to be wise,
Not even a potato of enormous size.
But if a potato were all I could be,
No potato on earth would be like me.

A SKELETON'S HOTEL

I learned a thing that's really scary,
That's made me jumpy, squirmy, wary.
Those skeletons we see each Halloween
Are also living with us in between.
(Between one October and another.)
Hiding inside father, mother, sister, brother.
Inside you and you and you and you.
(And I suspect inside me, too!)
My body is a skeleton's hotel.
It resides inside me very well.
Forgive me now if I scream and I shout.
I just scared myself from the inside out!

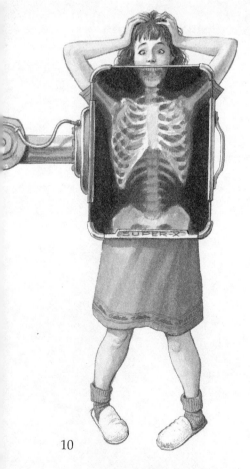

THE WART

A lie is like an ugly wart growing on your nose.
If you tell another lie, the wart will grow some toes.
After one *more* lie, the wart will not sit idly by,
Just tapping its toes on your nose, saying, "Oh, my!"
It will rise in indignation and walk off your face
And follow you around—here and there and everyplace—
Crying, "A Liar, Liar, Liar precedes this wart,
Dirty low-down liar, and most likely not too smart."
Every smart child knows that a liar is always caught
Whether he grows a wart with toes on his nose—or not.

WHY GOOD MANNERS MATTER

I like to lick my fingers
When eating ice cream or cake.
I like to lick my fingers
No big deal, for heaven's sake.
I like to lick my fingers
When eating salty french fries.
I like to lick my fingers
When I'm eating cherry pies.
I like to lick my fingers
—chocolate sauce, marshmallow goo.
I like to lick my fingers.
Now tell the truth—don't you?
I like to lick my fingers
When eating tapioca.
I like to lick my fingers
With cookies and hot cocoa.
I like to lick my fingers—
Ah, but now here is the rub:
I like to lick my fingers,
But all I've got left are stubs.

THE MONSTROUS BROCCOLI EXCUSE

You see, I don't like broccoli.
And broccoli does not like me.
It crawls into my room at night
Giving me a monstrous fright.

It scratches at the closet door,
Slithers-rustles across the floor.
This vegetable terminator
Has escaped the 'frigerator.

This isn't merely in my head.
It's really there under my bed.
Oh, Mom, how can I eat, you see,
A fearsome food that would eat me?

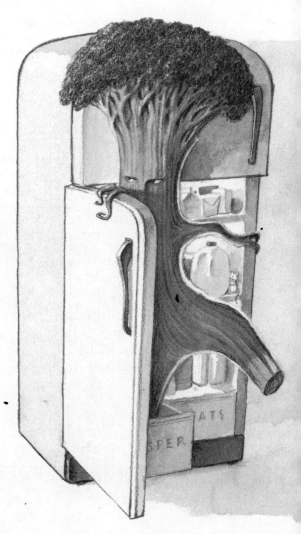

PEG-LEG ZEG

There was a pirate, Skeeter Zeg,
Who had a well-made wooden leg
That ended in an iron-capped peg.

One day he teased a crocodile.
Crocodiles are easy to rile—
They're only teased a little while.

Then Skeeter had two legs of wood.
Yet his brain didn't work too good.
He still did what he never should.

Zeg teased two big and nasty crocs
By pelting them with heavy rocks
And useless pairs of dirty socks.

Although crocodiles have their charms,
They're not as gentle as schoolmarms.
They made a lunch of Skeeter's arms.

The pirate's pegs then numbered four,
Yet still he teased the crocs some more.
I won't describe the gushing gore.

Zeg teases no more crocs. Instead,
He mostly stays at home, in bed.
He's got a fifth peg for a head.

He now does only the thing he should.
And his behavior is always good.
Guess he's smarter with a head of wood.

A SHORT TRIP

I'm in a funk.
I'm blue.
We went sailing.
Boo-hoo.
Set out for Spain,
We two.
But soon we sunk.
It's true.
No use bailing.
Oh, foo!
This is a pain.
Who knew?
You just can't float
A cardboard boat.

SILLY

Someone called me silly.
How very proud I am!
They could have called me mean.
They could have called me sick.
They could have called me geek.
They could have called me thick.
Someone called me silly.
I'm happy as a clam!
There's lots of boring stuff
To put up with in life,
Lots that's mean and nasty,
Much argument and strife.
Never enough silly,
And never will there be.
They could have called me skunk.
They could have called me rat.
They could have called me louse.
Or called me all of that.
Never enough silly.
I'm silly, yes, that's me.

THE PAPER DOORWAY

I lost myself inside a book last night.
Then found myself in a galactic fight,
A light-year out beyond the farthest star,
Driving a spaceship like a motorcar.

I fought giant spiders with eighteen feet.
As big adventures go, this one was neat.
Then the book fell shut while I was inside
And I escaped the things I can't abide:
Doctors and dentists, lima beans and school,
Homework, neckties, piano lessons, rules.
Everything was glorious, oh, so fine,
Out beyond where the very last stars shine.

Giant spiders were in foaming rages,
When Mother found me between the pages.
Oh, why did Mother have to come and look
Where I was happiest—inside my book?

ALL FAMILIES ARE NOT THE SAME

My father is a clown.
My mother is one, too.
His face is green and red,
While mother favors blue.
Each wears a silly hat,
Also a frizzy wig.
You can't help but notice
Their shoes are really big.
When we go to the mall,
The movies or the zoo,

I'd be most embarrassed
Were I not a clown, too.
We drive a little car,
Much tinier than yours.
Always we get tangled
Just getting out the doors.
Our noses honk if squeezed.
We're always falling down.
We have a lot of fun—
That's life if you're a clown.

MY WORDS

It is delicious to make up words,
So much tastier than whey and curds.
The words are mine when I invent them,
But if you want, I'll let you rent them.

Purrfur is my word. Give me a pat.
Isn't purrfur a fine word for *cat*?
Guzzlegas—now that word is a star.
I drive a guzzlegas—my old car.

Kinkyslink—a caterpillar. See?
'Cause it kinks as it slinks. Agree?
A *dinkytwink* is a distant star
You can barely see 'cause it's so far.

If toward potatoes you feel friendly,
You're a *spudbud*. If carrots send me,
Then I'll admit I'm a *bunnyfoodfool*.
But there's no nice word if you like gruel.

AUNTIE

If I go out, I'll be struck by lightning.
A thunderstorm is no safe place to be.
Staying inside is also frightening,
Because Aunt Winifred is here with me.

She's visiting us from Punxsutawney,
Staying seven days, which is forever.
She chatters and is fearsomely brawny
And wears an odd hat with a feather.

Maybe six thousand times every hour,
Auntie pinches my cheeks, and with a grin,
Says, "Adorable! You, I could devour."
It's as bad as if we'd let a werewolf in.

She smells like a big garden of roses.
Often I'm unable to catch my breath
When Auntie insists on rubbing noses.
I assure you, she will soon be my death.

She pats me on the butt and on the head
And tells me I'm the apple of her eye.
She says again what she's *already* said,
"You're so cutie-cutie-cute, I could cry."

She's always wanting hugs—and kisses, too.
I think I'm just about to lose my mind.
Sometimes I want to puke—and so would you.
Can't Auntie see my blush? She isn't blind.

The storm is growing stormier outside.
I'll take a chance with lightning from above.
No more, no more of this can I abide!
My Auntie Winifred is killing me with love!

THE MAN WITH FOUR EYES

I knew a man who had four eyes.
He claimed to be so very wise.
Two eyes in the back of his head
Closed only when he went to bed.
He saw much more than you or me.
A great wizard he claimed to be.
He saw ahead, he saw behind—
This, he said, improved his mind.
His claims I don't mean to deride
But the bus that hit him came from the side.

DOGS AND HOGS

If I could be a dog or a hog
I certainly would be a dog.
Nobody plays games with a hog.
And ham is not made from a dog.
Hogs are not taken to the park
To jump and run and play and bark.
Good dogs can sleep with you in bed.
Hogs wallow in the mud instead.
If I could be a frog or a hog,
I still would choose to be a dog.

WHAT I LIKE

I like the way snakes wiggle.
I like the way girls giggle.
I like the way rockets zoom.
I like the way fireworks boom.
I like the way monkeys swing.
I like the way church bells ring.
I like the way bluebirds sing.
I like almost everything.
I don't like folks who are glum.
Being glum strikes me as dumb.
I like folks who like life, too.
If you like life, I like you.

THEM AND US

I wasn't invited to the party.
Oh, I'll set loose some hungry wolves on *them*!
They're so very smart and so very arty.
Oh, I'll throw hives of bumblebees at *them*!
They'll all be playing games and having fun,
Till I stampede a herd of bulls through *them*!
They think they're so special, A-number-one,
They won't be special when I—

Wait.
Fate.
The mail was late.

Here's my invitation
To the celebration.

Oh, I've been invited to the party.
We are all so smart and very arty.
How sad that you should be so envious.
Not just everyone can be one of *us*.

THE YOUNG MUSICIAN—
OR MAYBE THUG

I want to play the drum, the drum!
The drum, drum, drum-a-drum, drum. Drum!
I've little talent, maybe none,
But I must play the drum, the drum!
Click, clack, and paddywhack—the drum!
Drum-a-drum, drum-a-drum, drum, DRUM!
Give me two sticks and a kettle,
And I will drum, drum on metal.
Drum-a-drum, drum-a-drum, drum, DRUM!
Give me two carrots and a table,
I will drum as best I'm able.
Click, clack, and paddywhack—the drum!
Drum-a-drum, drum-a-drum, drum, DRUM!
Give me two candlesticks of lead,
And I'll drum, drum, drum on your head.
If two sticks and drum you'll pay fer,
That certainly would be safer.
Click, clack, paddywhack—the drum!
Oh, I must play the drum, the drum!
Drum-a-drum, drum-a-drum, drum, DRUM!
Drum-a-drum, drum-a-drum, drum, DRUM!

HANDYMAN

Georgie can fix almost anything
With a little chewing gum and string.
He can fix a broken rocket ship
With a rubber band and paper clip.

He can fix every machine, it's true,
With wire and a drip-drop of glue.
Using no other tool but a fork,
He can fix 'em . . . but they just won't work.

MARY THINKS SHE WANTS A PUPPY

Oh, Mary had a little lamb.
But poor Mary wanted a puppy.
She traded the lamb for a ram.
Traded the ram for a guppy.

Traded the guppy for a duck,
And then with a little luck,
Traded for a magic fish
That gave her just one wish.
Mary wished for a little lamb,
Then said, "How silly I am!"

(She'd meant to wish for a puppy.)

Again she traded lamb for ram,
Then traded ram for guppy.
"Oh, dear, how clever I am:
I'm halfway to a puppy!"

But a cat ate the guppy,
So there goes the puppy.
No one would take the cat,
Because it was mean and fat.
"Now," said Mary, "here I am
With one mean cat, no lamb."

But on her birthday—"A puppy!"
So very furry and so cute.
Far more fun than a guppy—
But it chewed up Mary's boot.

It chewed up Mary's best hat,
Then chewed up the old mean cat.
She traded the puppy for a pig.
And this pig was hugely big.
For the pig, she got a rhino,
And the rhino was albino.

So finally, don't you know,
She got a lamb for that rhino.
Oh, Mary had a little lamb:
"I'm gonna keep it, yes I am!"

SAFE HOUSEHOLD ACCIDENTS

I fell right up the stairs
Instead of falling down.
I fell up to the top
And didn't break my crown.
Not easy to fall up.
It takes a little skill.
But it's much less painful
Than any downward spill.
Better try falling up
Next time that you tumble.
You won't break any legs
With an upward stumble.
And this advice as well:
There's less pain and clamor
Next time that you're nailing
If you use your thumb to hit the hammer.

FRANKENBUNNY

Thunder! Wonder!
Motion and commotion!

In the castle tower,
The monster-maker works.
At this scary hour,
Some evil beastie lurks.

Motion! Commotion!
Frightening lightning!

Lying on the table,
Made of bunny pieces,
It is not yet able,
To unfold its creases.

Oh, the windy wind!
Oh, the rainy rain!

The creature is crumpled,
Its eyes are bloody red.
It's gnarled and rumpled,
Strange stitches in its head.

Thunder crash! Lightning flash!
Organ music! Gloomy tunes!

Now it leaps to its feet,
Snarling, growling, groaning.
With a tail-twitch quite neat,
It stalks the night, moaning.

Frankenbunny! Frankenbunny!
Not a sunny little bunny!

Though its tail has waggage,
It has the urge to kill.
Wants to kill a cabbage—
I'm sure it surely will.

Frankenbunny on the loose!
Vegetables beware!

THOSE WEIRD GUYS IN NURSERY RHYMES

Jack be nimble, Jack be quick,
Jack jump over the candlestick.
If the candlestick was lit,
Jack must be a real nitwit.

Peter, Peter, pumpkin-eater,
Had a wife but couldn't keep her.
Oh, she was sickened half to death
By his perpetual pumpkin breath.

Wee Willie Winkie runs through the town,
Upstairs and downstairs in his nightgown.
Rapping at the window, crying at the lock,
"Are the children in their beds?
For now it's eight o'clock."

The children throw stones at him, and chairs
From their bedroom windows, all upstairs.
This busybody boy they all despise,
For without him they could watch TV
From now until sunrise.

A STRANGE DAY
ON THE FARM

Cows were howling.

Sheep were creeping.

Chickens were kickin' the dog.

Goats were gloating.

Ducks were clucking.

The cat just spat on the hog.

Horses were mooing.

Turkeys were cooing.

There's reason to feel alarm.

The corn is singing.

The wheat is ringing.

It's a strange day on the farm.

PLURALS

The plural of mouse is mice.
The plural of louse is lice.

So then shouldn't the plural of moose be meese?
Shouldn't the plural of caboose be cabeese?
After all, the true plural of goose is geese.

The plural of hippopotamus is hippopotami.
Then shouldn't two elephants be elephanti?

The plural of sneeze is sneezes.
The plural of cheese is cheeses.

So then shouldn't the plural of knee be kneezes?
And shouldn't the plural of one bee be beezes?
After all, the true plural of wheeze is wheezes.

Beside a field of grazing meese,
A train passed by with two cabeese,
Followed by stampeding elephanti.
Stampeding, and the reason why—
A pursuing swarm of angry beezes
Buzzing around elephanti kneezes.

The plural of mouse is mice.
I don't know why, but it's nice.

WISHES

I spend all my days making wishes.
It's much better than washing dishes.

I wish for money. And it might come.
And when it does, I won't be a bum.

Often I wish to be famous too.
When I'm a star, I'll still speak to you.

Sometimes I wish for a giant yacht.
I've wished for that giant yacht a lot.

I have wished for beauty and for brains.
I have wished for sunshine when it rains.

And if my wishes don't soon come true.
I'll have to wish for wishes that do.

BETTER THAN MONEY

Money I quickly spend.
Ice cream I gobble down.
Clothes I always wear out.
I'd rather have a friend.

Movies all soon end,
And trips out of town.
Rich food gives me gout.
I'd rather have a friend.

DINNER WITH JILLY

Jilly could never keep her room clean.
It was a dreadful mess.
She didn't like to play nice, either.
She caused us much distress.
She borrowed things she didn't return.
And now I must confess:
We baked Jilly in a big piecrust,
And ate her, more or less.

THE THREAT

I'm going to run away to Africa.
You see if I don't.
Maybe a family of apes will adopt me.
You think that they won't?
A family of apes adopted poor Tarzan,
Him just a baby.
I'm already half grown-up, you know.
I think that maybe
The apes will say it's a real good deal.
No diapers to change.

No tears, no fussy fits, no spitting up.
They'll surely arrange
To take me in, give me a fine ape name.
Maybe *Oompah-wook*
Or *Babba-juck* or *Heeba-goom* or *Goo-gack*
Or *Wampa-dook-dook*.
Lice thrive on hairy apes, or so you say.
I think lice are nice.
And every day I'll have to eat bananas?
So I'll eat 'em twice.
You say the apes also eat grubs and bugs?
So then I'll eat worms.
I'll adapt to the diet, I'll happily eat
Anything that squirms.
I'm going to run away to Africa.
You see if I don't.
Maybe a family of apes will adopt me.
You think that they won't?

Yes, I know I've packed twice before.
Never mind that, just show me the door.
The third time's the charm, never fear.
I'm off to the apes. I'm out of here!

YOU GET THE PICKLE YOU ASK FOR

She enjoyed feeling sorry for herself.
She had no pity for a trampled elf.
Not one tear for the family of the elf.
But she liked feeling sorry for herself.

She liked wailing, "Woe, woe, oh, woe is me!"
Weeping enough to fill up half a sea,
Being as sad as sad could ever be.
"Oh, poor, sad, sorry, hopeless, weeping me!"

She saw a troll be run down by a bus,
But she didn't moan or make any fuss.
When a gnome got shot by a blunderbuss,
She said, "Oh, well, he wasn't one of us."

A leprechaun was eaten by some bears.
The lady exclaimed, "Oh, who really cares?"
A pixie was beaten by thuggish hares.
But the lady just watched and ate eclairs.

So the elves bought a truckload of pickles
And ran her down, which gave them the tickles.
To buy the truck, they spent all their nickels,
But they giggled as they ate the pickles.

THE PRETTIEST BUTTERFLY
I WILL EVER SEE

I saw a butterfly,
Yellow and fleet.
It hit Dad in the face—
Wow, it was neat.
Baby brother flipped it
With his new spoon.
One pat of soft butter
At lunch, at noon.
Center of Dad's forehead—
A nice *ker-splat*.
Lunch was pretty funny
After all that.

I DON'T SHARE

I do not care to share
Baubles, rings, anything—
Ice cream, cake, or candy,
Anything that's dandy.
I don't share toys with boys.
Girls, too, can stay away.
What's mine is mine, is mine.
We'll get along just fine
If you have enough stuff

To play the day away,
And never ask to share.
I think that's only fair.
I am *pleased* to share peas,
Kidney stew, and the flu.
My lima beans are yours,
My brussels sprouts and more.
Don't go away. Let's play.
What's wrong with you? The flu?

DANGEROUS MUSIC

Playing a tune on his nose flute,
Ned accidentally inhaled.
Then a hard sneeze and one loud toot,
And Johnny was almost impaled
When the silly nose flute flew free
With a squeaky, shrieky tone.
There will be no nose flute for me.
I prefer the nuclear trombone.

A BAD CAT

Our kitty can't tell wrong from right.
He never learned to be polite.
He never went to kitten school.
He never learned the Golden Rule.
He stole my mama's brand-new car,
Although he didn't get too far.
Arrested near Cincinnati.
Cops said he was truly bratty.
We didn't have to post his bail,
'Cause cats are never sent to jail.
Now cat is in an ugly mood,
And, oh, he's being super rude.
He used my father's credit card
To order sixteen tons of lard.
Cat has no need for *any* lard,
They piled it out in the front yard.
Cat bit the mailman on the nose.
He tore up all my sister's clothes.
The family dog is terror struck
Of being run down by a truck—
Yes, driven by the family cat.
Oh, drat, this cat is quite a brat.

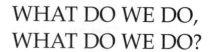

WHAT DO WE DO, WHAT DO WE DO?

There's a mouse in the house!
Do we burn the place down?
There's a mouse in the house!
Do we get out of town?

There's a mouse in the house!
Do we use dynamite?
There's a mouse in the house!
Do we all die of fright?
There's a mouse in the house!
Do we buy fifty cats?
There's a mouse in the house!
Do we all just go bats?
There's a mouse in the house!
Do we live in the yard?

There's a mouse in the house!
Do we hire a guard?
There's a mouse in the house!
There's a mouse in the house!
There's a mouse in the house!
There's a mouse in the house!

Wait a minute.
Unless I'm dreaming.
The mouse just fled
from all the screaming.

BASEBALL IS SAFER

Ned entered a cow-throwing contest.
Oh, he tried to do his very best.
He threw a Holstein about ten feet.
The Holstein let out an awful bleat.

The crowd cheered loud, and Ned took a bow.
The problem now was one ticked-off cow.
The cow got right up, shook off some dust,
Then snorted a hard, hot, angry gust.

The cow threw poor Ned 'bout half a mile—
A feat that made all the judges smile.
Cow wanted to win—and threw with zest—
But this wasn't a *Ned*-throwing contest.

A BEVERAGE WITH ANTLERS

I like the taste of orange juice.

And I like the look of a moose.

However, I don't like moose juice,

Nor do I want an orange moose.

THE CABBAGE FEELS NO PAIN

I have a headache from thinking too much.
Can't even tolerate a feather's touch.
People all sound as if they're talking Dutch.
My head must be in a pterodactyl's clutch.

My skull has turned to mucky mush—it throbs.
My brain's coming out of my ears in gobs.
Spike-foot elves run inside my head in mobs.
My sinuses are stuffed with old corncobs.

I should be a carrot. They never think.
Or maybe a nice grapefruit—one that's pink.
I'd agree to be a cabbage in a blink,
Because this headache's pushed me to the brink.

Of course, vegetables get eaten for lunch,
Eaten for breakfast and dinner and brunch.
I could be bananas—one entire bunch.
But on bananas, too, people like to munch.

So maybe I'll just be a heavy old stone,
Lying on a forest floor all alone.
I'll be the dust of a dinosaur bone,
Blown to wherever the wind wants me blown.

Maybe I'll straighten my brain with a comb,
Smack my aching head with a big fat tome.
Or maybe I'll just stop writing this poem,
Swallow two aspirin and go straight home.

THE RELIABLE BUNNY

Pity the Easter bunny
For his job isn't funny.
Carrying a billion eggs
Is so tiring on the legs.
Also a billion baskets!
He blows out all his gaskets
With all the heavy lifting
And so much Easter gifting.
All that chocolate candy
Is really too darn handy.
He nibbles here, nibbles there,
He's a nib-nib-nibbling hare.
Chocolate ducks and chickens—
How fast his waistline thickens!
Easter Eve—he wasn't big.
Now—big as a moose is big!
Bigger than a bear is big!
Bigger, bigger, really BIG!

Monday morning, he must diet,
Eating food that isn't quiet:

Crunchy lettuce, carrots, too.
Now he's feeling really blue.
Chocolate tasted so much better.
But he can't fit in his sweater.
No chocolate now—only clover,
Well, if he can still bend over
To eat the clover so sweet.
He can't even see his feet.
However, in another year,
When Easter again draws near,
He'll once more be slim and swift,
Missing not a single gift.
He can't be slowed by rain or snow.
The bunny simply is a pro.

PEACE THROUGH HOPPING

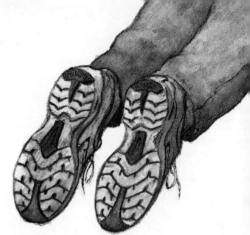

I have decided to hop.
Yes, no more walking for me.
Toads hop, frogs hop, rabbits hop.
Hopping is the thing, you see.
Crickets hop, so does the bird,
Not to mention kangaroos.
I give you my solemn word,
Although I will still wear shoes,
I will no more walk or stroll,
But hop, hop the livelong day.
To hop is my biggest goal,
And if I could have my way,
All of you would hop with me.
Oh, the world would be so nice—
Try hopping, and you will see—
You'll take my hopping advice.
You can't be mean when you hop.
You can't be angry or cruel.
You can't make war when you hop,
'Cause you look quite like a fool.

DO TREES SNEEZE?

Do trees sneeze?
I've heard them whisper
In the breeze.

Do trees sneeze?
I've heard them murmur.
Tell me please.

Do trees sneeze?
I've heard them gossip
With the bees.

Do trees sneeze,
Do you suppose?
And if they do,
Where is their nose?

THE SEASONS OF A TOAD

'Tis spring!
The stream has overflowed.
'Tis spring!
And I'm a toad.

'Tis summer!
The garden must be hoed.
'Tis summer!
And I'm a toad.

'Tis autumn!
Leaves blow across the road.
'Tis autumn!
And I'm a toad.

'Tis winter!
Oh, it has snowed and snowed.
'Tis winter!
And I'm a toad.

STARS, MARS,
AND CHOCOLATE BARS

Somewhere nearby a little bee
Is making honey just for me.
Somewhere a night bird peeps,
And his song puts me to sleep.

On hot days, the brook is cold.
On cold days, the fire is warm.
The rain is silver, sun is gold,
Blue sky is lovely—so's a storm.

In some strange land far away,
Beans are growing, and one day
They will become chocolate bars.
Beans turn into chocolate bars!

The night sky is full of stars.
And one day, I might go to Mars.
Stars, Mars, and chocolate bars,
Red bicycles and racing cars.

The world is filled with wonder
Inside, outside, above, and under.
This whole world was made for me,
Why, then, be anything but happy?

RAIN

I like rain in August,
Steaming on the street.
And I like rain in May,
When the air is sweet.

September rain is fine:
Helps the trees to grow.
December—I decline:
Christmas, we need snow!

October is frightening,
On a rainy night,
Thunderboom and lightning
—but also a delight.

March rain is an army,
Sounds of drum and gun.
And June rain can charm me,
Waiting for the sun.

I like rain that drizzles,
That pops and sizzles.
And I like rain that pours,
Gushes, rushes, roars.

SNOWLAND

On one bright summer afternoon
I set out walking to the moon.
I never made it half that far.
I should have driven in a car.

As I was walking down the street
I felt a grate beneath my feet.
A strange black hole was in the grate.
Too late, I noticed it too late!

In the grate was a cold dark space,
An open, gaping, empty place,
Between the bars, a gap so wide
I slippery-slipped down, inside.

Before I could think what to do,
I had fallen completely through.
And when I landed far below,
I fell facefirst in fluffy snow.

Astounded, I rose to my feet.
Far above was the summer street.
Up there—blue sky, a sunny glow.
Yet here I stood in falling snow.

I had no ladder, rope to climb.
My watch was empty—out of time.
Here, it was neither day nor night.
Nothing about the place was right.

Big boot prints led away from me.
I followed them. I had to see
If maybe monsters lived down here
I must admit to a bit of fear.

Then arose a bitter blizzard,
As if conjured by a wizard.
In the storm I saw the features
Of a thousand evil creatures.

I thought of my mom and my dad,
And all the times that I'd been bad.
I promised if I made it through,
I'd be good and honest and true.

The raging storm passed, and I found
All the boot prints were clearly bound
Toward a village built all of snow
From the high streets down to the low.

Snow castles, palaces of snow,
Towers, spires wherever you go.
Arches, bridges—above, below—
All crafted out of sparkling snow.

Then stranger structures all of snow,
Having functions I couldn't know.
Even trees were sculpted from snow:
Snow, snow, snow, snow—ever more snow.

Music swelled, sweet bells and flutes—
Ring-a-ding-dings, rooty-toot-toots.
Rock-and-roll but also cool jazz,
Christmas carols with razzmatazz.

Then in the village square I saw
A sight that made me gape in awe.
A fine orchestra of snowmen:
Drummers, horn players, and bow men.

Thousands of snowmen, all grinning,
Were singing, dancing, and spinning:
The jitterbug, waltz, fandango.
Others were trying to tango.

They tapped and kicked their dancing feet,
And they could really keep the beat.
They were jolly, round, and hearty.
Clearly they all liked to party.

Some wore top hats, some wore berets,
Or straw hats meant for summer days.
Some wore scarves, but others did not.
One wore a hat that was a pot.

Some were dapper. But some were hicks.
Some had arms of snow, some had sticks.
One had Christmas-tree bulbs for eyes,
And one wore a Santa disguise.

One boasted a shoe-brush mustache—
That gave him a lot of panache.
Rope made such handsome reggae braids.
Here was a cool cat wearing shades.

With coal or carrots for noses,
Some struck ridiculous poses.
Here was a band, there a combo.
Some danced conga, others mambo.

They capered and romped and rollicked,
Made merry, cavorted, frolicked.
I must admit some were coolish,
But most of them just looked foolish.

Their heads, of course, held only snow,
Not any brains—what could they know?
They knew enough to slip away
At first sign of a warm spring day.

You think snowmen melt into slush?
Big sloppy puddles of cold mush.
One of them told me, with a wink,
This is what they want you to think.

The truth: Snowmen don't melt away.
They go down to Snowland to play.
And none will come back here until
The first nippy new winter chill.

RUMOR

I heard this rumor, I know it's true.
Now I'd like to pass it along to you.

I heard about this school somewhere,
And what I heard will curl your hair.
At this school, the kids are strange.
Some might even say deranged.
Is it true that one of them grows
Little mushrooms between her toes?
Is it true that one of them keeps
An alligator with which he sleeps?
Is it true they eat chocolate sauce
Over mashed potatoes mixed with moss?
True that all these little dickens
Ride to school on giant chickens?
Well, all this sounds weird to me,
So someday soon I must go see
Their giant-chicken parking lot
And eat chocolate potatoes—*not*!

If every rumor proved to be true,
What would we do, what would we do?
No sailor would ever be safe at sea,
For giant, toothy serpents there be.

Ships would always be under attack
By sea serpents in need of a snack.
Alien monsters from out of the stars
Would be snatching us out of our cars,
Taking us home to put in their zoos,
Or cooking us up in their tasty stews.
If every rumor proved to be true,
What would we do, what would we do?

CRIME AND PUNISHMENT

When I brag, my eyes sag.

When I pout, my teeth fall out.

When I fight, my ears alight.

When I cheat, I get itchy feet.

It's pretty clear to see:

Mom's put a curse on me.

WALLY THE WEREWOLF

Wally is a werewolf
He prowls each moonlit night.
Wally is a werewolf
But doesn't like to bite.
Wally is quite hairy
And makes a fearsome sight.
For a wolf, however,
Wally is too polite.
He will not rip and tear.
He says it isn't right.
He is softly spoken
And much too nice to fight.
On some moonlit evening
Just maybe you will sight

Wally on a hilltop,
Flying his homemade kite,
Or on his unicycle,
Pedaling with all his might.
Werewolves laugh at Wally
And say he's not too bright.

But Wally won't be shot
On some deep moonlit night
By a silver bullet
Just for flying a kite.

A CURE FOR UGLY

There was a man named Barney Mugly.
None in the world was half as ugly.
A glimpse of Barney made brave men scream.
Barney belonged in a bad, bad dream.
He turned weak souls to stone with a smile.
His eyes were eerie. His teeth were vile.
Dogs whimpered when he wiggled his nose.
And Barney Mugly wore *ugly* clothes.

His ears were ugly, so was his chin.
His head was too fat, his thumbs too thin.
His tongue was too long, his lips too green.
His knees were hairy, his toes looked mean.

They made a movie of Barney's life:
How he longed for children and a wife,
Was a friend to animals (had a pet perch),
Was kind to neighbors and went to church,
Wrote poetry and baked tasty pies,
Was smart and funny and very wise,
Gave to the poor, visited the sick,
And built an orphanage brick by brick.
Barney did all this without one boast,
But the movie told everyone coast to coast.
Now thousands visit Barney's resting place,
And all treat him with respect and grace.
Each of the visitors always cries,
Standing where Barney forever lies.
Before the movie, they misunderstood.
They saw the ugly but not the good.
Now Barney's gone, no one can confuse
How pretty he was, played by Tom Cruise.

PRINCESS WITH A TAIL

I have a dog named Trixie.
She's as cute as a pixie.

Each morning I brush her an hour.
Once each week she receives a shower.

I serve her kibble by the scoop.
With plastic bag, pick up her poop.

After each walk, I wash her paws.
I brush the teeth in her big jaws.

I buy her treats, I buy her toys.
I let her play with girls and boys.

Easy to see why sometimes she forgets
Exactly who is master, who is pet.

WHY I FIND IT SO HARD TO LEARN

This morning, six-eyed bug aliens were on the school bus.
They ate Jim alive with ketchup but spared the rest of us.

During our reading class, Bigfoot broke in through the door,
Gobbled Mike, and used Sally Ann's head to mop up the floor.

A dinosaur peeked in a window while we kids studied math.
A huge, grinning, green *T. rex*, badly in need of a bath.

The coatroom has not one window to vanquish the vampire
Who lives—and lurks—in there amidst all the kids' attire.

On my report card, Teacher said I daydream, but I don't.
I just see the stranger things that others can't—or won't.

THE SHARK IN THE PARK

What a grand time I had in the park.
Well, except for the shark.
Flying my kite and throwing my ball . . .
Will the shark eat us all?
The park has a pond but don't look there,
Sharks can be anywhere.
Under a rock or high in a tree,
Right behind you—or me.

Sharks are so tricky, sneaky, and sly.
Dad can't understand why,
When watching for sharks, I scan the sky.
They say sharks cannot fly.
But sharks have been here millions of years,

So it's not strange to fear
That in so much time they learned some tricks
And perhaps get their kicks
From surprise attacks—ZOOM—diving down
Making not one shark sound.

Much stranger creatures than you and me
Live out there, wild and free.
Look at the duck, which both swims and flies
—or the owl, which is wise
But, though wise, nevertheless eats mice
Instead of something nice.
And, hey, what about the flying fish?
Sharks can't fly? Oh, you *wish*!

AT WAR WITH WOOD

An apple fell from a tree
And hit poor me.
Offended by this attack,
I hit right back.

So I broke my left hand,
And I broke my right knee,
But I taught that darn tree
Never to mess with me!

FOOD PSYCHOS

We have a turkey feast each Halloween.
On Thanksgiving Day all our food is green.
Every Christmas Day, it's hot dogs for us.
July Fourth, we eat oatmeal without fuss.

Oh, we're food psychos, food psychos we are!
We eat pints of mustard, straight from the jar!
Eat ice cream with a knife, soup with a fork!
Food psychos spread peanut butter on pork!

Throughout September we eat only bread.
In June we'll eat anything with a head.
In March we eat sandwiches of cactus,
Which requires tough gums and careful practice.

Yes, we're food psychos, food psychos and proud!
We eat anything weird, and we eat LOUD!
Hey, we're FOOD PSYCHOS! We'll even eat dirt!
We eat warm lima-bean mush for dessert!

BOOGEYMAN

Sometimes I hide under my bed because
The boogeyman has big teeth and claws,
And some nights he comes creeping back,
Searching for a boy-flavored snack.

He's evil, he's wicked, and he stinks.
Did you know that the boogeyman drinks
A ghastly brew that's made from bears
And bats and toads and witches' hairs?

He does, he does, it's true—and worse:
The fiend carries broccoli in his purse
And might make you eat broccoli stew
If he really, *really* doesn't like you.

He might stomp on you, squash you flat,
Then make you into a big rumpled hat,
And wear you on his strange, lumpy head.
Doesn't that make you shiver in dread?

He might make a necklace with your toes,
Decorate his key chain with your nose.
He might even make you shine his shoes
Or pay ten years of his video-club dues.

He might even disguise himself as you
And let your folks take *him* to the zoo,
To the movies, to the ice-cream shop
Where he'll eat and eat until he drops.

Meanwhile, you'll be locked in a box
With twenty-two pairs of his dirty socks,
With nothing to drink, nothing to eat—
Just the smell of the boogeyman's feet.

He's horrible, terrible, and nasty too.
There's no telling what he'll do to you.
He's got countless ways to get his kicks
In his big book of mean little tricks.

I must admit I've never actually seen
This master of mayhem, king of mean.
But around the corner he is lurking,
Planning new wickedness and smirking.

Who was it tracked mud in the house?
Not me, of course. It was that louse.
Who ate all the cake and the cookies?
Who hypnotized me into playing hooky?

Who made such a great mess of my room?
Who knocked over the vase with a broom?
Who spilled chocolate milk on the chair?
Who left a roller skate on the stairs?

The boogeyman, boogeyman! 'Twas him!
He's so wicked, evil, rotten, and grim.
The thought of him gives me a fright—
Though I thank God for him every night.

SICK

I am sick.

My head is thick.

I am ill.

I feel like swill.

I am faint.

Mouth tastes like paint.

I am queasy.

Tongue is greasy.

I am blurry.

Teeth are furry.

I am hot.

And then I'm not.

I am cold.

I smell like mold.

I feel sunk

In bogs of gunk.

Oh, so cruel—

I can't make school.

I can't make school!

I CAN'T MAKE SCHOOL!

Oh. So cruel.

Mom isn't fooled.

HEAD NUMBER TWO

My brother's from another universe,
If not from somewhere infinitely worse.
He's got two different heads and two brains—
No other theory properly explains
Why today he's nice, but tomorrow mean.
I suspect his alien heart is green.
I'm searching for the secret hiding place
Where Brother keeps his less-appealing face.
Soon as I find it, I will throw it out.
We'll both be a lot happier, no doubt.

ROCKS

Sue thinks rocks are for building.
Jan thinks they ought to be thrown.
Becky paints them with gilding.
Clever Tess sells them to Joan.
Joan piles them 'round her rose bed.
For Denise they're paperweights.
Pam makes gravestones for the dead.
Kay casts stones to read the fates.
So this much is very true:
Rocks have many more uses than
Might have first occurred to you.
Now we better talk to Jan.

RED HAIR

How I love the little girl with the red, red hair.
I like to follow her up and down and everywhere.
Sometimes I will just stand there stupidly and stare
At the perfect little girl with the red, red hair.

She follows a young boy with yellow, yellow hair.
I follow her as she follows him here and there.
I was angry when I saw the way she would stare
At the handsome boy with the yellow, yellow hair.

Then one day behind me, another girl was there.
A pretty little girl with auburn, auburn hair.
And in her eyes I saw a quite familiar stare—
The same stare I stared at the girl with the red hair.

Here is a girl who cares for me just as I do care
For the perfect little girl with the red, red hair.
It makes me quite happy to see this loving stare
From the cute little girl with auburn, auburn hair.

Now I see one thing I don't like, behind her there.
He is a smiling little boy with brown, brown hair.
Oh, these complications. I really must despair.
Why can't I be liked by the girl with red, red hair?

THINKING ABOUT ME

I think I will be tall.
Not short.
Not small.
Tall. Think tall.

I think I will be pretty.
Not plain.
Not giddy.
Pretty. Think pretty.

I think I will be smart.
Very smart.
With heart.
Smart. Think smart.

I think I will be kind.
Not mean.
But kind.
Kind. Think kind.

I think I will be happy.
Not sad.
Not sappy.
Happy. Think happy.

I think I will be whatever
I want.
Whatever
I want. Whatever.

THE FEARFUL BEE

I was afraid of ants
Crawling inside my pants,
Creeping into my nose,
My ears, too, I suppose.
Then I met a spider
When I sat beside her.
Ants aren't half as scary
As spiders—I was wary.
Any bug with eight feet
I did not want to meet.
One clear summer morning,
Without any warning,
I met a bee, a bee,
A bee, buzzing busily,
A bee! Buzzing at *me*!
A bee, a bee, a bee!
I ran fast, I ran far.
I passed a speeding car.
I ran until I dropped—
Stumbled, tumbled, plopped.
The little bee had fled
Back to his hive, and bed.
How can I fear a bee,
When I know it fears me?

THE BEAR WITH ONE GREEN EAR

Not once has this bear ever sneezed
On another bear's plate of cheese.
Not once has he ever thrown rocks
Or worn a pair of ugly socks.

When he finds a hive with honey,
He will share and take no money.
No, not one dollar, not one cent.
Green Ear is swell, a perfect gent.

He's never burped, been rude or mean,
When having luncheon with the Queen.
Crossing meadows in morning hours,
He avoids stomping on the flowers.

He won't growl at other creatures,
He has kind and bearish features.
Yet still his fellow bears will run,
When all he wants is to have fun.

They hide from him up in the trees,
Where some of them are stung by bees.
They hide from him under the rocks
And inside old grandfather clocks.

They disguise themselves as babies,
Clowns, car salesmen, and old ladies,
Hip musicians, old physicians,
Top-hat-wearing stage magicians.

They hope that he will pass them by,
And, yes, I know the reason why:
They think that he must be so mean,
Because of his one ear of green.

All these silly, frightened bruisers
Are the biggest bunch of losers.
Green Ear would be their bestest chum
If these darn bears were not so dumb.

TOAST AND JAM

I eat toast with lots of jam.
I eat eggs and I eat ham.
What I eat is what I am—
Toast and jam and eggs and ham.
I search the mirror to see
Where the jam is part of me.
I hope I shall *never* see
The pig that is part of me.

BALANCE

Fell down.
Got up.
Went on.
Fell down.
Wobbled.
Tottered.
Fell down.
Hurt butt.
Crawled some.
Got up.
Fell down.
Skinned knee.
Who cares?
Mom's shoes
Are fun.

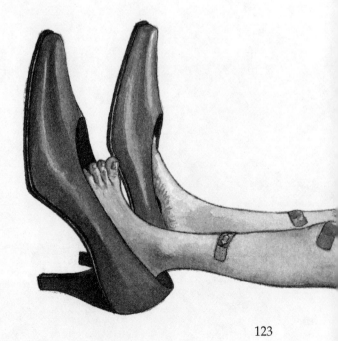

WHY MOST PEOPLE
PREFER CATS AND DOGS

My grandpa gave me a dinosaur.
Dinosaur snores
Rattled the floors
And shook the doors.
And dino's burps
Broke window glass.
We won't discuss
His passing gas.
Dino's head cold
Was quite a mess.
Got it from me,
I must confess.
One giant sneeze
Knocked Mama down
And, oh, the snot

Ruined her gown.
He ate two cows
Each day at noon.
And chickens, too,
A whole platoon.
Sweet though he was
He had to go.
How sad it was
To lose dino.
Hauled him away,
Off to the zoo,
Where he passed gas,
Killing two gnus—
One elephant,
Two deer, one ape,
Seven big snakes,
Four jackanapes.
The zoo sent him
Back to Grandpa,
Where the neighbors
Viewed him with awe.
He didn't bark,
Bite like a shark,
Howl in the dark.
But Grandpa lives in a trailer park.

125

FASHION-PLATE FIDO

The dog is always in fashion,
In winter, spring, summer, and fall,
Though for clothes he has no passion,
And always wears nothing at all.

CATS IN SPATS

Cats do not like to wear hats.
They refuse shoes, also spats.
Offered some fine, fancy boots,
Cats always turn up their snoots.

I glimpsed a cat in a tutu once.
Oh, he was a silly-looking dunce.

Cats do not like to wear socks,
Elegant and frilly frocks.
They rebel at scarves, mittens—
Even when they're just kittens.

I saw a cat in a lacy stole.
A dog ate him on a whole-wheat roll.

THE AGES OF A TOAD

I recall the tadpole stage.
Lovely wriggly-squiggly days.
Never had to earn a wage.
I could swim a long, long way.

Got my legs too soon, too soon.
Carefree tadpole days were done.
Now I hopped under the moon,
And that, too, was lots of fun.

School was held on lily pads.
We learned to squeak and ribbet.
We caught flying bugs—oh, scads—
And danced the fibbergibbit.

With school behind, I set out
To become a traveled toad.
Pond life was nice, have no doubt.
But still this toad hit the road.

I worked as a lumberjack,
Chopping down hundred-foot trees.
This played havoc with my back,
And tree pollen made me sneeze.

For two months, I drove a cab.
And, oh, how I liked to speed.
But some folks wouldn't pay the tab.
When I drove too fast, they peed.

Gave parachute instruction
To Chinese restaurant chefs.
Discovered by deduction—
Very little rhymes with *chefs*.

I saw Paris and New York,
Fibbergibbited in Spain.
Fell in love in County Cork
But ribbeted all in vain.

She I loved did not love me.
My song never won her heart.
But I got one kiss, hee-hee.
For playing the prince's part.

Then I came to middle age,
And felt the urge to perform.
In Shakespeare I strode the stage.
Dare I say, a star was born?

My movies are all big hits.
I'm a famous toad, you know.
My fans swoon in fevered fits,
Cast red roses where I go.

You'll soon see me in *Ben-Hur*
Riding chariots in Rome.
Then I play an eskimo
In deep snow north of Nome.

So far middle age is great,
But old age will be better.
In fact, I can hardly wait
To wear my old-toad sweater.

To sit in my rocking chair,
On my green lily-pad rug,
And eat chocolate eclairs—
I long ago gave up bugs.

Every sunset will be mine.
At sunrise I'll rise and shine.
Every day will be sublime
In this toad's life that is mine.

LISTEN TO THE WIND

Listen to the wind!
Hear it spin, spin, spin!
Telling where it's been:
Rome and back again.

Listen to it howl!
Hear it growl, growl, growl!
Wind is on the prowl
And it wants in now!

Listen to it sigh!
Hear it cry, cry, cry!
Such a sorry sigh.
Don't you wonder why?

Listen to it moan!
Hear it groan, groan, groan!
Such a gnawing tone,
Hungry for a bone.

Listen to it climb
Through the bright wind chimes,
Keeping time, time, time:
Music so sublime.

THE PIG WITH PRIDE

I once found a pig in my blanket
Settled comfortably in my bed,
Its big snout down beside my two feet
Its little tail curled next to my head.

I ordered the pig to get out at once
And to go back to sleep in its sty.
It wuffled and snuffled and huffled—
And instead of moving, it asked, "Why?"

Politely I explained: "Pigs like mud,
Not beds—not houses, but open sky."
The pig wuffled, snuffled, and huffled—
And instead of moving, said, "Not I."

"You're not a good pig," I then accused.
"It's breakfast time. Now go to your trough."
The porker wuffled, snuffled, huffled.
"I much prefer a table," it scoffed.

"What next, what next, you silly swine?
Will you want to wear my pants and shoes?"
The swine wuffled, snuffled, and huffled
And said, "I look best in greens and blues."

Are you surprised that I sympathized
With the piggie and its desires?
Each of us wants to improve himself
And have dreams to which he aspires.

I dressed Pig in my dressiest best.
And stuffed his feet in four fine boots.
"You look very handsome," I declared.
Pig said, "One day, I'll own *many* suits."

Then breakfast. (Not a word of bacon.)
Grapefruit, cereal, toast, and jelly.
Foreboots off, Pig was good with a fork.
"This," said he, "is how to fill a belly."

"Now kind sir," I said, "we're off to class."
And Mr. Pig said that would be cool.
The gentleman wuffled and snuffled:
"Yes, you can't get ahead without school!"

UP

I've got nowhere to go but up.
I'm just a pup.
I can climb up to the sky.
    I'll tell you why:
   I'm shiny new, just starting out.
     I feel a shout
         Coming on. Oh, I'm just a kid.
        There is no lid
           On top of me. No chains at all.
           I may be small,
              But I've nowhere to go but up.
                I'm just a pup.

AN ANGRY POEM
BY A DRAGON'S MOTHER

The kindly dragon of Foogamaloo
Could play the piano and the kazoo.
And if you want more story, shame on you.
What more do you want a dragon to do?
So many music lessons, so much time,
And it cost dragon far more than a dime
To become a musician so sublime.
Criticizing him is clearly a crime.
Can *you* play the piano and kazoo?
And if you say that you can play them too,
I've another question to ask of you:
Do you have big claws? I don't think you do.
Try playing the piano with big claws.
And do you have enormous toothy jaws?
Hard to toot a kazoo without flaws
When you have his enormous toothy jaws.

Good grief! You really want too much, I think!
Your demand that he do more just . . . well, stinks.
You know he could breathe out fire in a wink
And cook you until you're tender and pink.
Time to give dragon some applause, I think.

AN ACCIDENT AT THE POLE

Santa Claus might be late this year
Because an elf fell in his ear.
Prying the elf out of his ear,
Claus backed into a big reindeer.

With antlers tangled in his pants,
He launched into a frantic dance.
The deer broke loose of his caboose,
But Claus fell on a Christmas goose.

The angry goosey squawked and flew,
And the next thing poor Santa knew,
He had goose feathers up his nose
And goose poop on his black boot-toes.

His fancy suit now needs a mend,
So to the cleaner's he will send
The clothes he needs to wear that night.
'Cause Claus won't fly till he looks right.

AN INTERESTING FACT ABOUT DOGS

Every doggie walks upon its toes
Here and there and everywhere it goes.
Not flat on its paws, but on its toes,
Wagging its tail and twitching its nose.

Do your research and then you will see:
Dogs are far different from you and me.
No doggies can play concertinas,
But some might become ballerinas.

One day your dog might dance a ballet.
He might be superb—or just okay.
Even kings would come from far away
To see your doggie dance a ballet.

If ballet is too hard for your mutt,
Then possibly he could sway and strut
Through a swing dance to a hot combo
Or catch a Latin beat, do a mambo.

Toe-walking dogs could certainly dance,
Win competitions from here to France,
But dogs don't care for competition.
They have talent but no ambition.

LUCKY SKUNK

A skunk is a lucky fellow.
No one is ever rude to him.
Because he doesn't smell mellow,
He need never go to a gym.
He can be as soft as Jell-O,
Yet even a bully quite dim
Will offer a friendly "Hello!"
And never pick a fight with him.

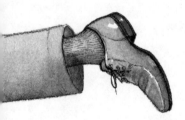

SO THERE

If I were a bird, I'd never fly.
If I were a spy, I'd never pry.
If I were a cow, I'd never moo.
If I were a ghost, I'd never boo.
If I were an owl, I'd never hoot.
If I were a horn, I'd never toot.
I'm stubborn, and there you are.
I wouldn't drive if I had a car.
I wouldn't eat if I had ice cream
—not even Chocolate Fudge Supreme!
I wouldn't sled if there were snow.
If a movie's good, I just won't go.
I'm stubborn under stars and sun.
I'm stubborn, though it's never fun.

HORSE THIEF

He was a real horse thief,
Full of mayhem and mischief.
His color was dapple.
He stole an apple,
A bottle of Snapple,
And galloped out the door,
A criminal now forevermore.

A LONG DAY OF RHYMING

A cop goes on a stakeout.

A prisoner plans a breakout.

A baker takes the cake out.

A mechanic checks the brakes out.

A barbecuer cooks his steaks out.

A counterfeiter puts the fakes out.

A Californian rides the quakes out.

A gardener brings the rakes out.

A hungry man orders takeout.

A snake charmer lures the snake out.

A proofreader casts mistakes out.

A hunter searches the drakes out.

And this poet has finally flaked out.

INSULTS

I called the girl a blister
'Cause she made me very sore.
She is my little sister.
And she often is a bore.
She said that I make her puke,
That I'm meaner than the flu.
I was hurt by this rebuke
'Cause I suspect it's true.

ADVICE

I want to give you some advice:
Don't drink poison, never eat mice.
Don't stomp scorpions without boots.
To sky dive use your parachutes.
Don't drink water from a toilet.
Talking in a movie spoils it.
Never give bugs as Christmas gifts.
Never wear shoes with yard-high lifts.
Don't ask a grizzly bear to dance.
Don't keep bumblebees in your pants.
Don't insult a rhinoceros
Or tell him he's preposterous.
Never sleep on a bed of nails.
Never chew scaly things with tails.
Your nose'll fall off if you pick it.
Cactus'll prickle if you lick it.
Well, I guess I might as well go.
Isn't this all you'll need to know?

BEING ME

It's such a lot of trouble being me.
Sometimes it wears me out.
Every morning I've got to take a shower.
Sometimes I sit and pout.
The me that I am is a showering person.
Mother has seen to that.

The me that I am eats breakfast, too—
A healthy one. Oh, drat!
I'd rather eat doughnuts, candy, cake,
But none of that for me.
It's cereal, fruit, and crisp dry toast.
Oh, how hard it can be!
The me that I must be dresses neatly.
Not rumpled or unclean.
The me that I am must comb my hair:
Always fit to be seen.
The me I've become must wipe my nose
The moment it is runny.
And brush my teeth and wash my hands.
Ah, this isn't funny!
The me that I call me must be polite
Even when I feel rude.
The me known to me as me must smile
And not get in a *mood*.
Being me is more than I can bear.
I don't know what to do.
I want to be rude, unclean, and sloppy—
Maybe I could be *you*.

THE WOGGLE WRANGLER

My name is Willard Dillard. I am a woggle wrangler.
With other woggle wranglers, I ride the range all day,
Chasin' down wild woggles and herdin' them together,
Which isn't easy 'cause woggles always want their way.

Cowboys wrangle cows, but cows rarely put up a fight.
And wranglin' herds of horses is likewise easy pay.
Woggles, on the other hand, are nasty, stubborn beasts.
When you try to lasso one, the woggle says, "No way!"

We wrangle in August heat and in the winter cold.
We wrangle all our lives, and we cannot get enough.
And when we fall asleep, we still wrangle in our dreams.
But even in our dreams, woggle wranglin' is darn tough.

A woggle has ninety teeth and forty-one sharp claws.
Woggles spit a rancid spit and spew a poisonous snot.
Woggles have a roar that will blast your ears clean off.
And they aren't gentlemen even after they've been caught.

Wranglin' woggles down in Texas, we lost fourteen men.
Since there were ten of us, it's amazin' I'm still here.
Sometimes woggles eat us like we're just corn on the cob,
Then wash down this grisly dinner with ice-cold beer.

My name's Willard Dillard. I been wranglin' eighty years.
I've caught ten thousand woggles and turned ten thousand loose.
In light of all my sweat and tears, that may seem real strange:
But the problem is that for woggles, no one's ever found a use.

Nobody wants to eat 'em, 'cause they taste worse than mud.
No horseman will dare saddle them—not even on a bet!
Their gnarly hides make ugly clothes that no one will wear.
Rancid spit, poison snot—a woggle's not much of a pet.

Yet still I wrangle through the years, happy wranglin' man,
Ridin' the range, chasin' woggles, in the blazin' sun.
There's no darn money in it, and not much common sense—
But I'll wrangle till I die, 'cause I'm havin' so much fun.

WHY?

My favorite pastime is wondering why.
Why is it blue up there in the sky?
Why not green, yellow, chartreuse?
Why do birds fly—but not one moose?
If a moose could fly, why not sing?
Oh, what a lovely, wonderful thing—
A moose that could fly and sing.
And if he could sing, why not dance,
Up on a stage in red-sequined pants.
What a very famous moose he would be.
People would come from miles to see
Him fly, sing, and dance all in red.
And why not balance mice on his head?
A pyramid of five happy white mice,
Each of them juggling grains of rice.
He would be a rich and famous moose.
He'd buy a train with a gold caboose.
And if he happened to be my friend,
We would travel around every bend
To magical places both near and far,
Eating doughnuts in the dining car.
Across the plains and over the hills,
With endless adventures and thrills,

Every day happy and full of delight,
With laughter and music every night.
And all this because I wondered why:
Why is it blue up there in the sky?

POEM BY MY DOG

Woof. Woof-woof-woof-woof.
Arf. Wuf-wuf, arf-wuf-moof.
Snort.

Grrrrrr. Woof-woof. Snuff.
Ack, ack, ack, ack. Wuf-wuf.
Snort.

Slurp. Slurp, slup, slurrrrp.
Woooooof. Slurp, slup. BURP!
Snort.

Owwwooooooooo!
Owwwooooooo!
Owwwoooooooo!
Owwwooooooo!
Snort.

Every picture in this book
Contains a mouse: Take a look.
Some are hidden, some are bold.
Some are babies, some are old.
We like mice. We don't like rats.
Mice are nice, but rats are—<u>rats</u>.
We could have hidden elephants
By putting them in funny pants
And baggy sweaters and old hats.
Or we could have hidden cats.
We could have hidden armadillos
By disguising them as pillows.
We could have hidden slimy worms
And other creepy things that squirm.
We didn't want to leave you sick,
By hiding what makes you say, "<u>Ick!</u>"
So all we've hidden are the mice.
'Cause Mr. Parks and I have lice.
Oops! In my rhyming, I was confused
And now Mr. Parks is not amused.
Mr. Parks and I do not have lice.
I meant to say that we're too nice
To make you search for worse than mice.

INDEX